raccoon

Cottonwood
Populus deltoides

Poison Ivy
Toxicodendron radicans

Horse Chestnut
Aesculus hippocastanum

snake

Caitlyn & Jonathan

Trees Talk!

Susan Coolidge

The Stories Trees Tell

Fact, Fantasy, and Fun

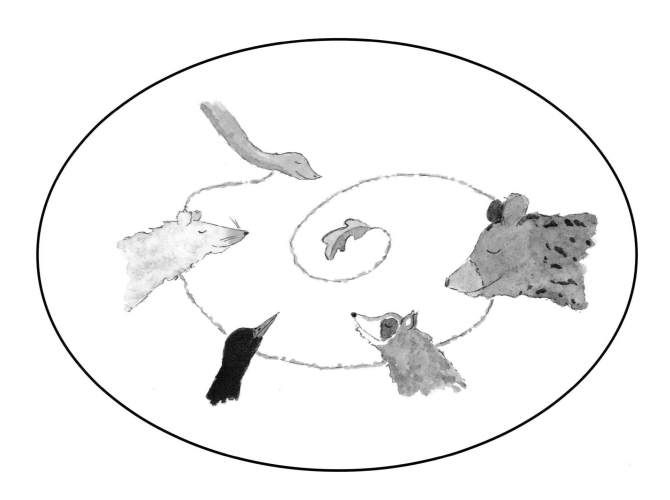

Written and Illustrated by

Susan Coolidge

Banjo Dog Press

Connecting Children and Nature

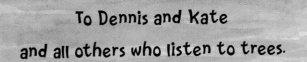

To Dennis and Kate
and all others who listen to trees.

© 2009 by Susan Coolidge

All rights reserved. For more information, contact Banjo Dog Press at www.banjodogpress.com.

Coolidge, Susan, 1944-

   The stories trees tell : fact, fantasy, and fun / written and illustrated by Susan Coolidge.

      p. : ill. ; cm.

   Summary: An interactive nature storybook featuring animal friends who travel through five different habitats and learn about trees in interesting but unusual shapes. Contains tree facts and learning activities for children.

ISBN: 978-0-9801448-0-2

1. Trees--Juvenile literature. 2. Trees. I. Title.

QK475.8 .C66 2008

582.16

LCCN: 2007941055

Printed in Korea

3 5 7 9 8 6 4 2

Banjo Dog Press
Connecting Children and Nature

20 Lowell Street   Cambridge MA 02138
www.banjodogpress.com

"Hello, my name is
Woodpecker and here
are my friends:

Opossum,

Snake."

Black Bear,

Raccoon,

Introduction

"Trees, trees, trees! Like you, all of us live with trees, and trees grow almost everywhere: in cities, in towns, in fields, and in forests.

"Do you know that trees are storytellers? During their long lives, trees have adventures, and these adventures leave many clues behind: missing parts, scars and holes, and strange branch and trunk shapes.

"Some trees have such unusual, magical shapes that you may think something unnatural has happened to them. But if you befriend a tree and get to know it, you will hear the story it has to tell.

"Come with us to meet our tree friends; they have such interesting stories. Let's first imagine how they came to have fantastic shapes, and then they will tell us their true stories. So grab your imaginations, and let's get going!"

3

A Country Road

A tree is a tall woody plant, usually over 10 feet tall.

Trees can be

single-stemmed,

or multi-stemmed.

Every year trees grow taller and their twigs, branches, and trunks grow thicker.

The leaves, twigs, and branches make up the "crown" of the tree.

"Meet my friend Chestnut Tree. Look at how her trunk splits and grows sideways. What could have happened to her?"

4

crown

leaves

twigs

branches

trunk

roots

Tree roots spread out even farther under the ground than the branches do above.

As a tree ages, its twigs grow larger and become branches.

Throughout a tree's life, its branches always remain at the same height above the ground.

The same tree in 1950 and in 2020

So, a swing that hangs on a branch that is 10 feet above the ground in 1950 will still be 10 feet above the ground in 2020!

Over time a tree's lower branches usually die and fall off.

roots
rootlets
root hairs

Roots connect to smaller roots, called rootlets. Rootlets connect to root hairs that absorb water and nutrients (minerals) from the soil.

5

"Hssss—Listen to ME! I know that Chestnut Tree's upper branches broke when the Thunder Kittens dropped a ball on her crown."

"Hmmm. My guess is that the upper branches broke off when an Apatasaurus used Chestnut Tree to scratch her tummy."

"W-E-L-L N-O-W—Looks like a napping tree. I always break off the top branches when they poke my back."

"Hey, hey, hey!!! I imagine that Chestnut Tree lost her upper branches when a gigantic bird took them to make her nest."

"Reader, why do YOU think Chestnut Tree is shaped like this?"

Trees can be divided into three groups: deciduous [di-sij-oo-uhs], evergreen, and palm.

Deciduous trees lose their leaves in the fall, and new leaves grow in the spring.

Persimmon trees, oak trees, and ash trees are all deciduous.

persimmon

white oak

green ash

Deciduous trees can be called "hardwoods" because their wood is hard.

8

Fully grown deciduous trees can have as many as 200,000 leaves during a season!

Worldwide there are over 80,000 species (kinds) of deciduous trees.

Some trees are evergreen, which means they remain green all year.

Pines, firs, and spruces are evergreen trees.

Needle-bearing trees are called "softwoods" because their wood is relatively soft.

"Wow! Your imaginations are amazing, but here is my true story. I began growing eighty years ago, and I quickly grew to the telephone lines. During one spring storm, my highest branch snapped the lines, and the next day the repairmen came by to cut me down. The neighborhood children, who made tiny jack-o'-lanterns from my chestnuts and jumped in my leaf piles, ran up and down the road telling everyone what was happening. The neighbors gathered under my branches and refused to let the repairmen and their saws get anywhere near me.

"In the midst of all the yelling and shouting, a little girl, named Mary Lou, insisted that just the top of my trunk be cut off and the rest of my branches left alone. Everyone cheered when the repairmen agreed. So the top of my trunk was removed and that just pinched me a little. With the tallest part of my trunk gone, my side branches grew up high around the wires but didn't touch them. So this is the story of why I have such a different and interesting shape! If you keep your eyes open as you travel along streets and roads, you will see many fantastically shaped trees like me, all trimmed to avoid the wires above them."

These are evergreen leaves:

hemlock,

pine,

and arborvitae.

Some evergreens also have another name. Because of their cones, evergreen trees like pines, firs, and spruces are also called conifers.

Cone— Con-i-fer

There are over 550 species of conifers in the world!

Palms, which all live in warm climates, also remain green all year.

The leaves of palm trees are called "fronds."

palm frond

palm frond

9

A City Park

Austrian pines are evergreens.

The leaves of evergreens trees do not fall off all at once, so the trees remain green all year. Hence, their name.

Instead of falling all at one time, some needles fall off every year and new ones grow at the growing tips.

The needles on evergreen trees are actually leaves, and like all leaves, they make food for the tree.

Evergreen leaves are thicker than deciduous leaves; this helps keep water inside so they have it available to them all year long.

"Here is my friend Austrian Pine Tree. Wow! He is split into four trunks, but his pine tree neighbor only has one trunk. What on Earth could have happened to him?"

Kato Park #

Evergreen leaves are either needles (pine),

or scales (arborvitae),

or spines (cedar).

The seeds of the evergreen develop inside the pinecone.

cones closed and open

Cones are covered by small overlapping plates called scales.

scale with winged seed

Seeds form under the scales, and when the time is right, the scales open to release the seeds.

hemlock seeds

Each tree produces many cones and hundreds or thousands of seeds.

The seeds are small and light and are easily carried by the wind.

AUTHORIZED VEHICLES ONLY

Cones come in many different sizes.

Hemlock cones are only about 1 inch long.

The sugar pine cones can grow up to 20 inches!

At almost 5 pounds, the Coulter pine's cone is the heaviest of all. Watch your head!

"Hssss—Listen to ME! This isn't a pine tree at all. Four of my friends are doing tailstands on a post!"

"Hmmm. My guess is that Austrian Pine's trunk split into four pieces when Woolly Mammoth stepped on him by mistake!"

"W-E-L-L N-O-W—Looks
like Comet dropped her comb
when she was untangling her tail.
When the comb hit the Earth, it
started to grow!"

"Hey, hey, hey!!! I imagine that this is
really a saguaro cactus that got lost
far from his desert home. Then he
grew bark to keep himself warm!"

"Wait, wait, Reader, what do YOU
think happened to Austrian Pine?"

A tree's trunk is made up of several layers (see the drawing at the bottom of the page).

1) The outer bark protects the wood from weather, hungry animals, and disease.

2) Inner bark, or phloem [flow-um], is the layer where the tree's food, called sap, is carried in tiny tubes to the growing parts of the tree.

3) Cambium is the layer of the trunk that produces cells for the new growth of the roots, branches, and trunk.

4) Sapwood is made up of tiny tubes that carry water and minerals from the roots to the leaves and other parts of the tree.

14

5) Heartwood is the hard, dead, inner core of the trunk that supports the tree.

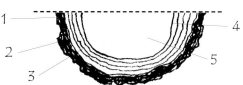

cross-section of a tree trunk

Every year as a tree grows, it produces another growth ring.

If you count these rings, you can determine the tree's age.

How many rings can you count?

A thick growth ring means a good growing year while a thin ring indicates that the tree was stressed that year.

A tree may be stressed by drought, bugs, or other animals , including people, or by weather, fire, or competition from other trees.

Tree Knots:

(See the drawings below.)

a) A new branch grows out from the trunk.

b) As the tree ages, new wood forms around the base of the branch.

c) If the tree is cut into lumber, you can see where the branch was growing through the trunk.

d) A knot in wood indicates where a branch once grew.

"Howdy! Your stories are wonderful, but my true story started about seventy years ago. One spring two old gardeners planted me in this fancy garden by the ocean. I grew happily until I was about seven feet tall. Then one winter there was a terrible ice storm that left an inch of ice over everything: roads, stone walls, bushes, and all of us trees.

"The old oak tree across the path from me was badly damaged by this storm. He struggled to hold up his ice-crusted branches, but he just couldn't support the weight of all the ice. In the middle of the night there was a loud crack, and one of his largest branches crashed down right on top of me!

"I was very surprised, but not badly hurt. The top of my trunk had snapped off, but then the four highest branches that remained grew up toward the sun and became four new trunks. So now, lucky me, instead of having just one trunk, I have four!"

"Lucky ME!"

a

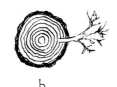
b

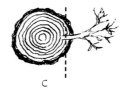
c

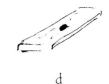
d

how a branch of a tree becomes a knot in a board

A Nature Trail

Trees need food in order to grow and make new bark, roots, leaves, flowers, and seeds.

The tree's food is produced inside its leaves by chlorophyll, which is the green color in leaves.

Using the sun's energy, the chlorophyll separates the water in the leaf into hydrogen and oxygen.

The hydrogen is mixed with carbon dioxide (a gas in the air that enters the leaf through tiny holes, called stomata) to produce the tree's food and oxygen.

This food is called sap.

"Meet my friend Maple Tree. Look, he's got three holes in his bark, and none of the other trees do. What do you think has happened to him?"

The sap travels to the growing parts of the tree through tiny tubes under the bark.

Trees store their extra sap to nourish new leaves and flowers in the spring.

This food-making process is called photosynthesis [foh-tuh-sin-thuh-sis].

In the fall, there is less sunlight, and leaves stop producing food.

Then the chlorophyll fades and uncovers the red and yellow pigments (colors) in the leaves. Some leaves also produce an orange color.

When a layer forms between the stems and the twigs, the leaves fall to the ground.

Over time, the fallen leaves decompose (rot) and become food for their tree.

Humans breathe out the carbon dioxide that trees use, and trees produce oxygen that humans breathe in—it's a perfect balance!

Two mature trees can produce enough oxygen for four people!

Trees have many branches and twigs to hold the leaves up high to collect as much sunlight as possible.

"Hssss—Listen to ME! I bet my friends made these holes when they were playing hide and seek."

"W-E-L-L N-O-W—Looks like these are Maples Tree's eyes, and he watches out for all of the creatures on the Nature Trail."

"Hey, hey, hey!!! I imagine that three woodpeckers were racing through the forest, didn't watch where they were going, and crashed into Maple Tree!"

"Hmmm. My guess is that these holes were made by Unicorn, who used Maple Tree for target practice!"

"Reader, what do YOU think Maple Tree's story could be?"

How To Tap A Tree:

A tree must be 10 inches across or about 40 years old to be tapped.

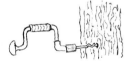

A hole 2 inches deep is drilled into the tree.

A spout called a spile is gently tapped into the tree and a bucket is hung under the spile.

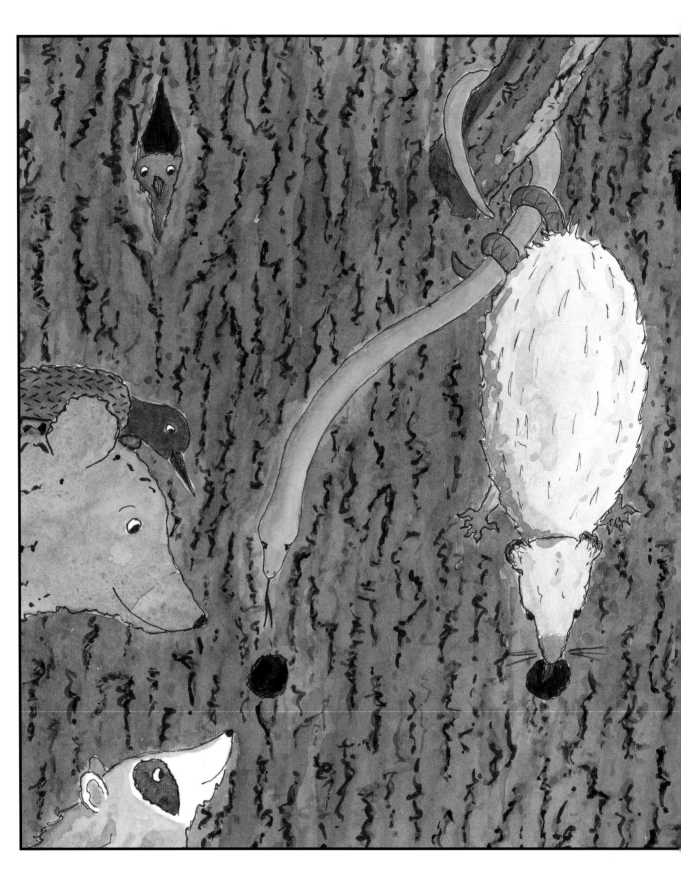

The sap drips out of the spile into the bucket.

The bucket is covered to keep out rain, snow, bugs, and thirsty deer and squirrels.

A sapscicle forms when sap, dripping from a broken twig, freezes.

Squirrels love sapscicles!

The boiling sap creates so much sticky steam that most maple syrup is made in special outdoor buildings called "sugar shacks."

There are usually holes in the roof to allow the sticky steam to escape.

Traditionally, sap was collected in buckets and brought in to be boiled.

"Hey down there, I want you to know that we were NOT properly introduced! My friend Woodpecker calls me Maple Tree, but I am not your ordinary, garden-variety maple tree. I am the sweetest and best of all the maples, and my full and proper name is Sugar Maple Tree. That line of small holes on my trunk was not made by fast-flying birds or playful unicorns or snakes. No indeed, those holes were drilled by a woman who wanted to collect my sap and boil it down to make syrup.

"My story is SOOO interesting, and luckily for you, I have nowhere to go. So gather 'round and hear my tale. My sap is a liquid that carries food to the growing parts of my trunk, branches, and twigs. Stored in my roots during the winter, this sap runs up and down in tiny tubes just under my bark. In the spring, with all of my sap on the move, it flows freely out of any hole or crack in my bark. So this is the best time for people to collect sap to make syrup.

"As long as not too much of my sap is drained off, I am not harmed at all. People have been known to make syrup from other kinds of maple trees and even birch trees. But it is well known that my sap makes the tastiest syrup of all!"

tubes

Now, many people collect sap by running a series of tubes from tree to tree. The sap flows through the tubes into one large container.

Once the sap is collected, it is boiled until most of the water has evaporated away and what remains is syrup.

an evaporator for boiling sap

40 gallons of sap boil down to only 1 gallon of syrup!

A Lakeside Beach

While not a tree, poison ivy can grow as a plant, a bush, or a vine.

Poison ivy leaves grow in groups of three.

The leaves can be 2–5 inches long and dull or glossy green in color.

In the spring, the new leaves are a shiny red, and in the fall they turn brilliant yellow, red, or orange.

Poison ivy has an oil in its leaves, stems, and roots that causes an itchy rash on the skin of many people.

This oil is called urushiol [yoo-roo-shee-ol] oil.

"My friend Cottonwood Tree lives here near the lake. But look at the gashes on her trunks. What in the world happened to her?"

"Hssss— This is Poison Ivy!"

Up to 70% of people get a rash from just touching the poison ivy leaves.

Urushiol oil stays active for up to five years—so even a dead poison ivy plant can cause an itchy rash!

You can even get poison ivy from patting a dog or cat that has been in contact with the plant.

Poison Ivy can be dangerous. People can become very sick breathing smoke from a fire that has any part of the poison ivy plant in it.

If you suspect you have touched poison ivy, wash thoroughly with strong soap and water as soon as you can. Wash your clothes before wearing them again.

Poison ivy was given its common English name by Captain John Smith when he came across it in the New World in 1609.

In the fall and winter, the white poison ivy berries provide food for many birds.

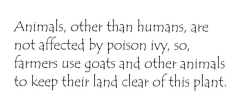

Animals, other than humans, are not affected by poison ivy, so, farmers use goats and other animals to keep their land clear of this plant.

Always remember:

"LEAVES OF THREE, LET IT BE;

BERRIES WHITE, DANGER IN SIGHT!"

23

"Hssss—Listen to ME! I know that Mouse used Cottonwood's bark to make himself a leaf boat."

"W-E-L-L N-O-W— Looks to me like Lion scratched off the bark while he was sharpening his claws."

"Hmmm. My guess is that Moon fashioned slippers out of Cottonwood's bark!"

"Hey, hey, hey!!! I imagine that a sea monster sprang from the waters and snacked on Cottonwood's trunks!"

"Reader, wait, I want to hear your story!"

During the summer, trees make buds that contain the flowers and leaves for the next year.

Overlapping scales protect the buds during the winter.

closed bud

As the weather warms up, the buds open and the flowers and leaves unfold and grow larger.

unfolding bud

Each tree has a different kind of colorful and/or sweet-smelling flower:

sugar maple flowers,

dogwood flower.

In order for any species to survive over time, it must reproduce, and trees reproduce by making seeds.

In a process called pollination, seeds are produced by the combining of the male and female parts of flowers.

Deep inside flowers is a sweet juice called nectar. Nectar attracts insects or other animals to flowers.

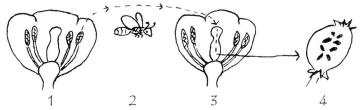

how pollen is carried from flower to flower

"Yes sir, Raccoon, you were right when you imagined that a sea monster sprang from the lake waters and attacked me! They are monsters all right, and they live in the lake behind me. They are brown and hairy with pointy webbed feet and large flat tails which make them fast swimmers. But scariest of all, they have huge, golden buck teeth that ripped and shredded and tore and gnawed at my beautiful bark and wood!

"These monsters found my trunks delicious, and they chewed two ENORMOUS holes in me. I was lucky they didn't chew all the way around my trunks! If that had happened, I would have died because that would have broken all the tubes that carry my food and water. These tubes are just under my bark. Hey, I've heard that humans have a special name for my monsters, but I don't know what it is! Do you?"

How Pollination Works:

1) As insects or other animals drink the nectar or eat the pollen, some of the pollen rubs off on their bodies.

2) Traveling from flower to flower, animals carry this pollen (male part) to other plants.

3) Some of the pollen rubs off on the pistil (female part) of the new flower. This pollen travels down through the style into the ovary, where it fertilizes the ova (eggs). They become seeds.

4) The ovary swells as seeds develop. This is called the "fruit" of the plant or tree (see the drawings above and below).

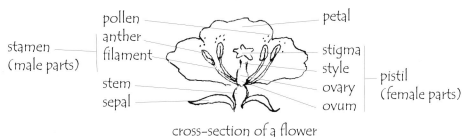

stamen (male parts)
pollen
anther
filament
stem
sepal
petal
stigma
style
ovary
ovum
pistil (female parts)

cross-section of a flower

A Northern Woodland

Fruits can be juicy like an apple or a berry, or they can be dry like an acorn or a chestnut.

juicy

dry

A drupe is a juicy fruit with a central seed called a pit. Cherries and peaches are drupes.

A nut is a seed inside a hard shell.

acorn

A key is a dry fruit with a flat wing or wings for traveling with the wind, like a maple seed.

sugar maple

A pod encases several seeds.

catalpa

28

"Meet my friend Paper Birch. Look at the base of her trunk. It is so different from the other birches around here. What could her story be?"

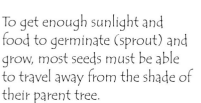

To get enough sunlight and food to germinate (sprout) and grow, most seeds must be able to travel away from the shade of their parent tree.

birch

Wind carries some seeds.

cottonwood seeds

Some seeds travel by water.

coconut

sprouting mangrove seed

Animals also move seeds. When they eat fruits, some whole seeds pass out in their feces.

Of all the seeds that animals eat, only a very few survive to germinate in a good growing place.

Scientifically, only plants with flowers produce fruits, so peppers and pumpkins are fruits, but not coconuts or pinecones!!

burr

Some seeds, called hitchhikers, have little hooks that catch onto animals' fur. Then the seeds are scattered when the animals move to another place.

beggar tick seed

29

"Hmmm. My guess is that too many party balloons were tied to Paper Birch's branches, and they lifted her half way out of the ground!"

"Hssss—Listen to ME! I bet Giant wanted to use Paper Birch's roots as a toothbrush, but he couldn't pull her trunk all the way out of the ground. So poor Paper Birch, her roots were left half in the soil and half out!"

"W-E-L-L N-O-W—Looks like the trees were practicing their branchstands, and Paper Birch got stuck upside down!"

"Hey, hey, hey!!! I imagine that Dragon pulled the branches down to make herself a nest, and then the branches grew down into the ground!"

"Hey, Reader, what do YOU think Paper Birch's story could be?"

The tallest trees on Earth are the Redwood trees in California.

Some of these trees grow up to 380 feet tall!

This makes then as tall as a 30-story building.

They are 5 stories taller than the Statue of Liberty which is 306 feet tall.

In other words, redwood trees are TALL!

The heaviest tree on Earth is a giant sequoia tree in California. Named General Sherman, it is 273 feet tall and its truck is 35 feet around.

This tree contains enough wood to build 120 houses, but luckily it is protected and will never be cut down.

dwarf willow tree

2 inches

The world's smallest trees are the tiny dwarf willows that live in the Arctic, where it is VERY cold! Full-grown, these trees are only about 2 inches tall.

The Bristlecone pine trees in the western United States are believed to be the oldest trees on Earth. Some of them may be over 5,000 years old.

This means that they started growing before the Egyptians built the pyramids!

But most trees don't live more than a few hundred years.

"Hello there! Your ideas are wonderful, but my story is even more startling. Sixty years ago I was just a tiny seed blowing hither and yon in the wind. I finally drifted down, but I didn't land on the ground. Instead I settled into the loose soil on the upturned roots of a fallen hemlock tree.

"That would have been bad news for most seeds, but not for ME. I can grow almost anywhere! So I sent out my tiny roots and they started to grow right there on top of the fallen tree's roots. I was pretty high off the ground so my roots had to grow extra long. They grew down, down through and around the hemlock's root ball until they reached the soil. As I grew taller and taller, my roots became thicker and stronger. Now so much time has passed that the hemlock has completely rotted away, leaving me standing on tippy toes, or should I say tippy roots?"

Aspen trees, which live in the west, are interesting trees.

They reproduce by forming sprouts called suckers from their roots.

As these suckers grow into new trunks, the old trunks die off.

So, aspens are made up of trunks and sprouts, and this is called a colony.

One aspen colony named "Pando" is estimated to be 80,000 years old!

But the bristlecone pines are still considered to be the oldest living single trees.

seed

1   2   3   4

"Thank you for walking with us and sharing the trees' stories. Now turn the page for more tree fun!"

Befriend a Tree

Getting Started

Thank you for walking with us and learning to hear the stories trees tell. Now for fun befriend a tree, get to know it well, and you will learn the stories that your tree has to tell. Here are a few projects to help you get started. When you study your tree, you will become a dendrologist [den-drol-o-gist], which is what a tree scientist is called!

Dendrologists keep all of their information in a notebook, so you will need to find a notebook or a scrapbook. You could even just staple a dozen or so blank pages together to make your own book! As you collect information about your tree, record it in your book and be sure to date each page. Scientists always do this!

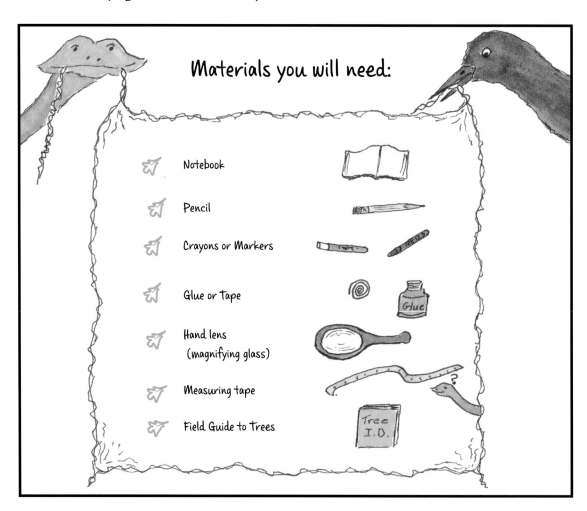

Materials you will need:

- Notebook
- Pencil
- Crayons or Markers
- Glue or Tape
- Hand lens (magnifying glass)
- Measuring tape
- Field Guide to Trees

Find a Tree

First hunt for a tree that interests you: a tall one, a short one, a crooked one, or one with unusual bark or shapes or holes. Look in your backyard, in a nearby park, or in the woods.

When you have found your tree, say hello and give it a big hug, but, first make sure it has no poison ivy growing on it!

Your Tree's Shape

◇ Stand back and study the shape of your tree from all sides. Is it a circle, a triangle, or something else?

◇ Walk around your tree and look up at its branches—do they grow up or down or out?

◇ Now look up and find a large branch. Walk away from your tree until you are exactly under the tippity end of that branch. The roots of your tree grow underground even farther than this from the trunk!

◇ Now draw a picture of your tree in your notebook and be sure to include lots of details.

The Circumference of Your Tree

Remember, trees grow out as well as up, so dendrologists are interested in the circumference, or distance around the trunk of a tree.

Using a tape measure—or string and, then, a ruler—measure the distance around the trunk of your tree.

⬧ Measure at your shoulder height or about 4 feet off the ground.

⬧ To double-check your measurement, ask a friend to measure your tree also.

⬧ Record this measurement in your notebook.

⬧ As you visit your tree over the years, continue to measure and record its circumference. As a tree ages it grows more slowly—just like you!

The Height of Your Tree

Chances are you are not tall enough to reach to the top of your tree to measure its height. Here is a way to get that measurement without even using a ladder!

◇ First, measure the height of a friend and stand him/her next to your tree's trunk.

◇ Now back away so you can see the whole crown (top) of your tree.

◇ Hold a stick upright at arm's length and look toward your friend.

◇ Slide your thumb up until the part of the stick above your thumb matches the height of your friend.

◇ Holding your thumb steady, move the stick up the tree to see how many times the top part of your stick fits into the height of your tree.

◇ Now multiply that number by the height of your friend. For example, if you count 5 stick lengths and your friend is 5 feet tall: 5 X 5 = 25, and so your tree is about 25 feet tall.

◇ To double-check your measurement, switch places with your friend and have your friend do the measuring while you stand next to your tree.

◇ Record this measurement in your notebook.

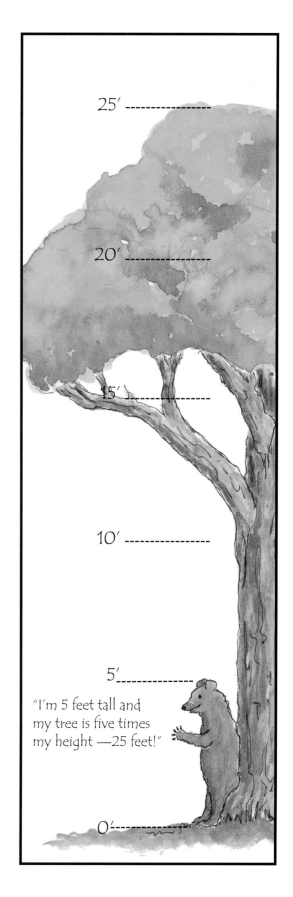

25' ----------------

20' ----------------

15' ----------------

10' ----------------

5' ----------------

"I'm 5 feet tall and my tree is five times my height —25 feet!"

0' ----------------

Your Tree's Leaves

Check under your tree and find a leaf—or needles or scales if you have chosen an evergreen. Remember, needles and scales are leaves too, just different shapes. Take a close look at your leaf.

If your tree is deciduous (its leaves fall in the fall),

◇ What is your leaf shaped like?

a hand?   a heart?   an oval?

a feather?   or something else?

◇ How does your leaf attach to its stem?

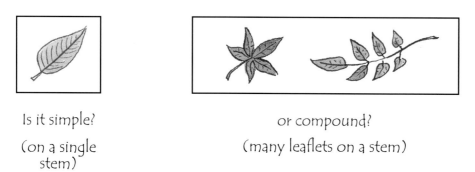

Is it simple?   or compound?
(on a single   (many leaflets on a stem)
stem)

◇ Examine your leaf's edges. How would you describe them?

smooth?   lobed?   toothed?

- Some trees are evergreen (their leaves do not all fall off in the fall). Can you tell if your tree is evergreen? You may know this already or you may have to observe it over the course of a year.

- If your leaves are needles, are they in bunches of

     2's?   3's?   5's?

- Measure the needles. How long are they?

"3 ½ inches!"

- Other shapes of evergreen leaves are:

  scale-like,   single needles,   simple with spines.

Studying Your Tree's Leaves with Your Hand Lens

- Do you see a pattern in the arrangement of your leaf's veins? Veins carry water and food.

- Do you see any holes or spots? If so, what do you think might have made them?

- Draw your leaf in detail, adding veins, stem, all the colors, holes, and spots you see. Date your drawing and add it to your notebook.

- You could also do a leaf rubbing or put clear contact paper on both sides of your leaf to preserve it.

Your Tree's Bark

⋄ Now give your tree another big hug and notice how the
  bark feels. Is it smooth or rough or ripply or soft?

⋄ How many different colors can you find in the bark?
  Look carefully up and down and use your hand lens to get an even
  closer look.

⋄ Now check: does the bark look the same on the branches
  and the trunk? How is it different?

⋄ Finally, draw your bark in detail or make a bark rubbing. To
  make a rubbing, place a piece of paper over a section of bark
  and rub it with the long edge of a peeled crayon.

⋄ Glue or tape your bark drawing or rubbing into your notebook.

There are many kinds of bark. Be careful not to hurt the bark on trees;
peeling it off can harm the tree.

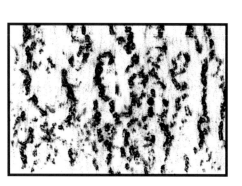

scales

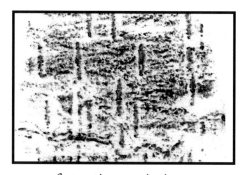

flat with straight lines

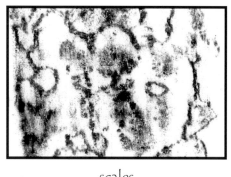

ridges

smooth

40

Your Tree's Flowers

When spring comes, look for your tree's flowers. Look carefully because tree flowers can be tiny. If you find a flower, study it with your hand lens and discover how many different parts a flower has! (See page 27.)

◇ What colors, parts, and shapes do you see in your flower?

◇ Does your flower have a smell?

◇ Draw your flower and paste your drawing into your notebook.

Your Tree's Flowers Become Fruits and Nuts

The flowers develop into fruits that contain the tree's seeds. The fruit can be juicy like an apple or a berry or it can be dry like an acorn or a maple seed. Look on the ground and on your tree for its fruits. Remember that the fruit may be in the shape of a pod or a hard ball, so look closely. When you find a fruit, study it carefully.

⬦   Is your fruit juicy or dry?

⬦   What colors and shape is it?

⬦   Does it have a smell?

⬦   Are there signs that someone has been nibbling on your fruit? Who could it have been?

⬦   Now draw your fruit, then open it up to look for the seeds and draw what you find inside.

If yours is an evergreen tree, you may see small cones on the tree, some of which will grow larger and become the woody cones that contain the tree's seeds. Look around near your tree and see if you can find last year's cones.

⬦ Use your hand lens to study your tree's cones, and draw a detailed picture of one of them for your notebook. Can you find seeds in the cones?

Your Tree's Story

Congratulations! By studying your tree carefully, you have become an official dendrologist! Using this information, you can look in a field guide for trees and identify what kind of tree your friend is. But first, it is time again for telling stories.

◇   Walk around your tree and look for clues of the adventures your tree has had: holes, bumps, scars, and unusual shapes.

◇   Sit under your tree, close your eyes, and imagine what wondrous things might have happened to your tree to create its interesting shape.

◇   Make your story as fantastic, magical, and silly as you'd like.

Next, close your eyes again and listen very carefully. You will hear sounds like the rustling of leaves, the swishing of grass, and the twittering of birds. In among all these sounds you will hear the softest of voices, and that will be your tree telling you its true story. Because you have become such good friends with your tree, you will be able to hear what it has to say.

Now open your eyes and decide how you would like to record these two stories. In your notebook you could:

◇ write the stories down,
◇ draw pictures illustrating the stories,
◇ write a poem about the stories.

Or you could tell the stories by:

◇ building a diorama or model;
◇ making a collage using some of the tree's leaves, seeds, cones, or bark;
◇ making up a play with your friends;
◇ creating a dance or a song;
◇ or whatever else you would like to do.

Finally, introduce your friends to your tree and share your tree notebook and stories with them.

Now that you have learned how to hear the stories trees tell, you will notice that every tree has its own special tale. On your tree walks, don't forget to visit your first special tree friend again and again to see how it changes over time.

Trees are our Friends!

- Trees produce much of the oxygen that we breathe.

- Trees use the carbon dioxide that we breathe out to make their food.

- Tree roots hold onto the soil so that it doesn't erode or wash away in the rain and wind.

- Trees help to keep the Earth cool by shading the ground.

- Trees provide protection from the sun's rays for animals, including us. We humans are animals!

- Trees' flowers, fruits, and seeds provide food for many living things.

- Trees provide homes for animals—under their bark, in their branches, inside their trunks, and in among their roots.

- Trees produce the lumber to make toys, houses, pencils, ships, furniture, popsicle sticks, and many other things.

- Trees are terrific for climbing on and playing in.

And—Trees have stories to tell!!!

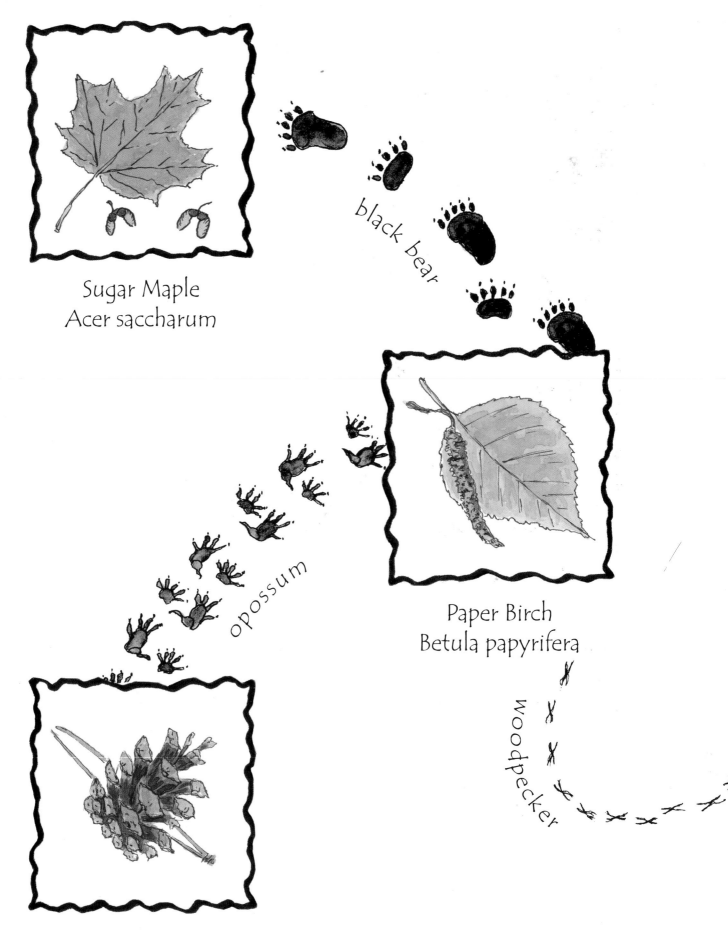

Sugar Maple
Acer saccharum

black bear

opossum

Paper Birch
Betula papyrifera

woodpecker

Austrian Pine
Pinus nigra